Saxophone Fingering and Scale Chart

By Eric Nelson

Fingering Chart: Saxophone

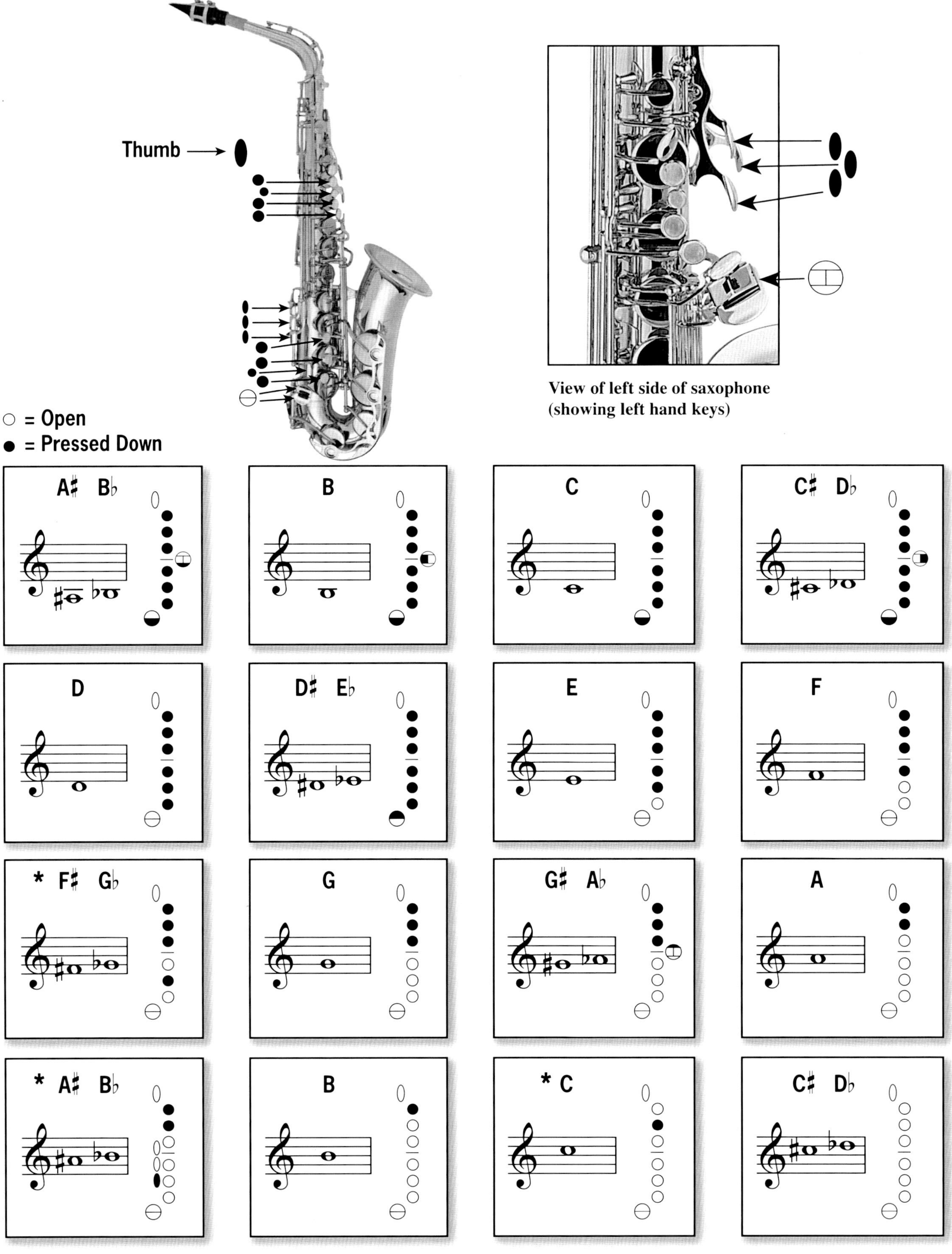

* See Alternate Fingering Chart

Fingering Chart: Saxophone (Cont.)

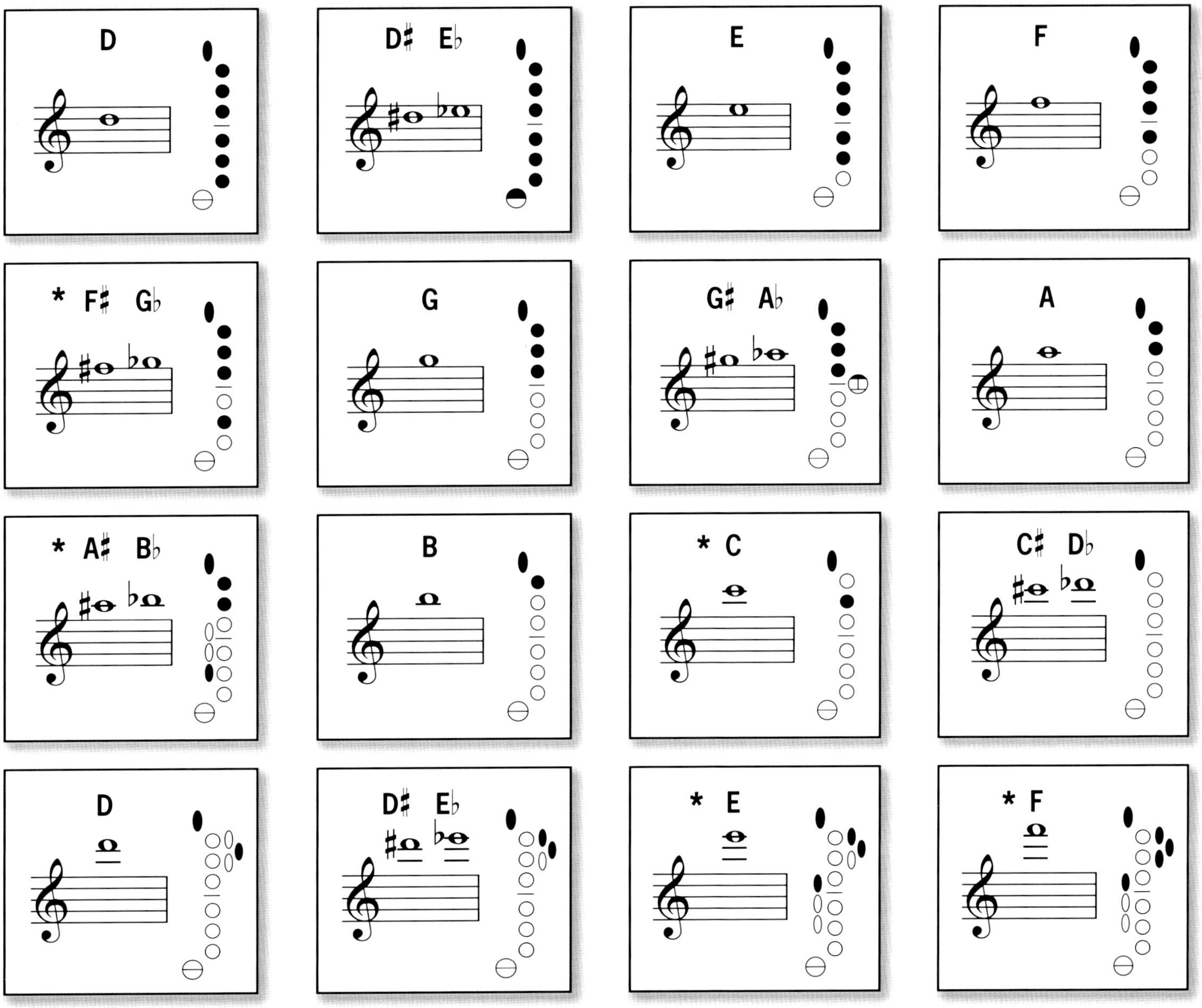

D
D♯ E♭
E
F
* F♯ G♭
G
G♯ A♭
A
* A♯ B♭
B
* C
C♯ D♭
D
D♯ E♭
* E
* F

*Common Alternate Fingering Chart

Alternate fingerings are used to make some note patterns smoother. These patterns are found in the scales and arpeggios on the back of this chart.

① F♯ G♭
② A♯ B♭
③ A♯ B♭
④ C
⑤ F♯ G♭
⑥ A♯ B♭
⑦ A♯ B♭
⑧ C
⑨ E
⑩ F

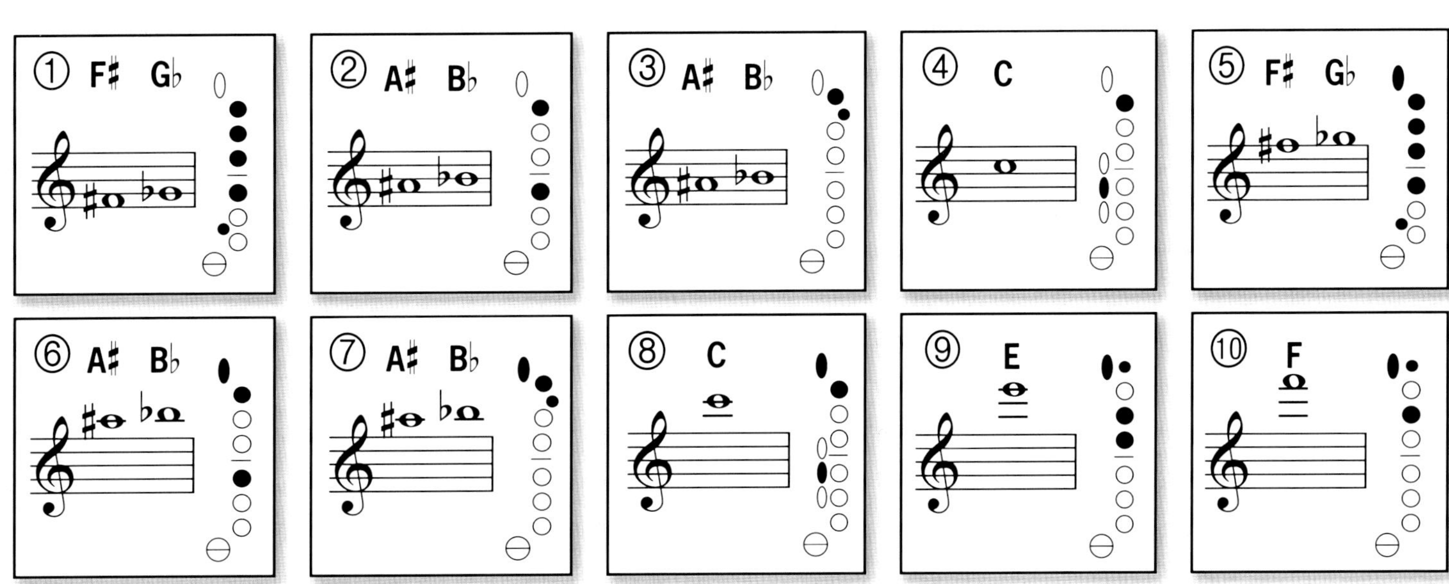

Major Scales and Arpeggios

Key of G (B♭ Concert)

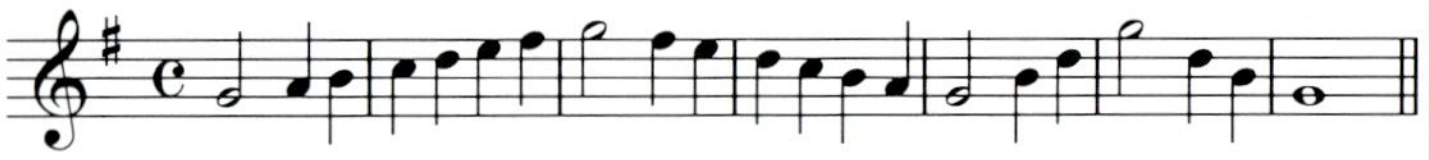

Key of C (E♭ Concert)

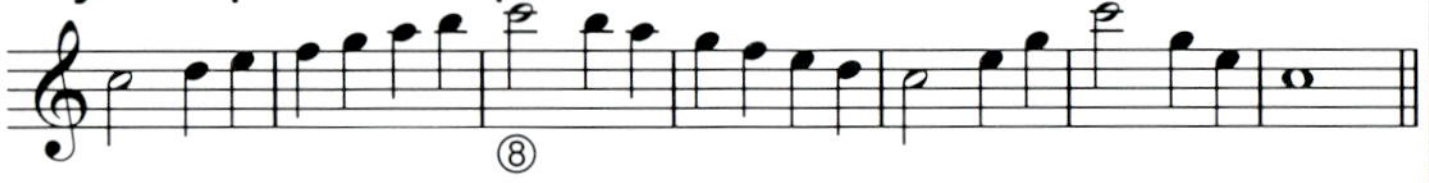

Key of F (A♭ Concert)

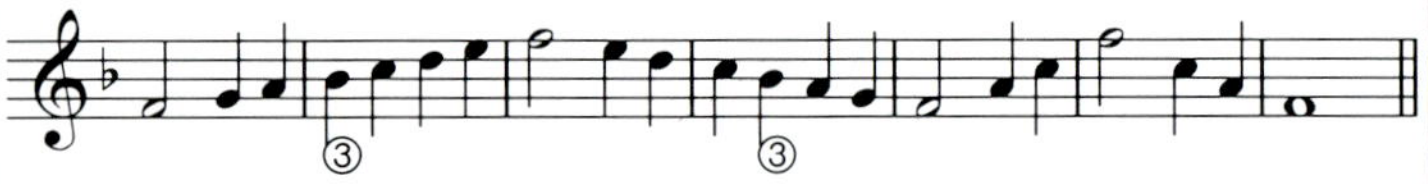

Key of B♭ (D♭ Concert)

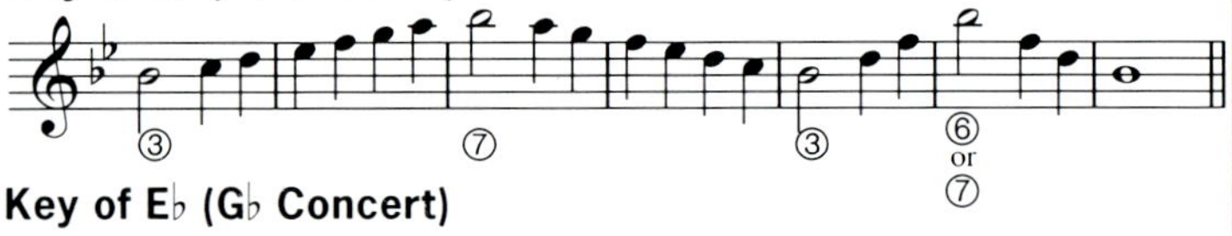

Key of E♭ (G♭ Concert)

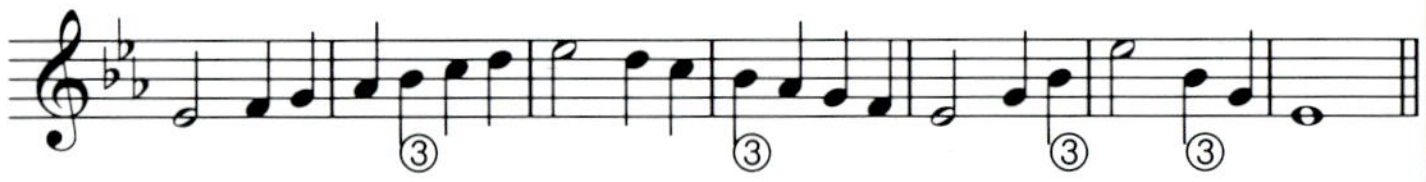

Key of A♭ (B Concert)

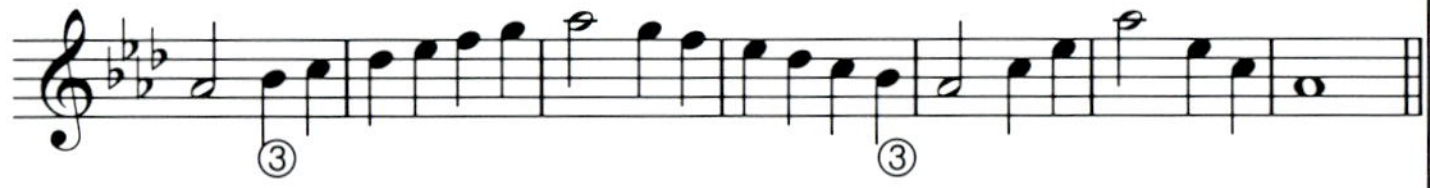

Key of D (F Concert)

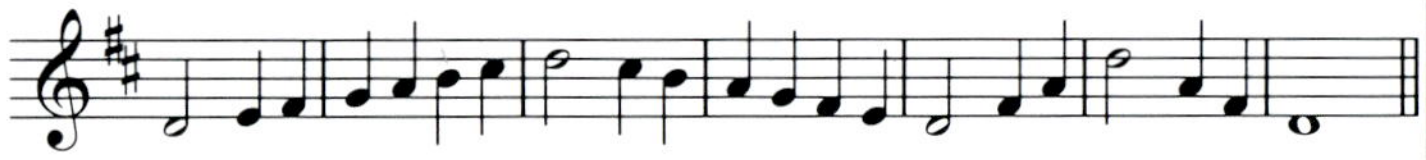

Key of A (C Concert)

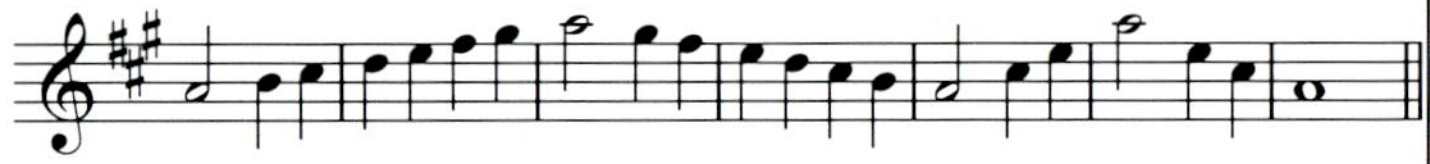

Key of E (G Concert)

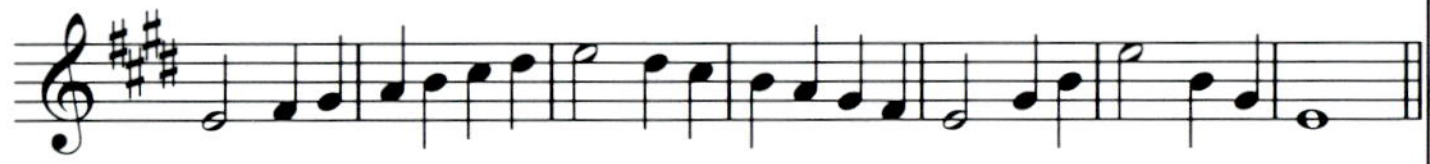

Key of B (D Concert)

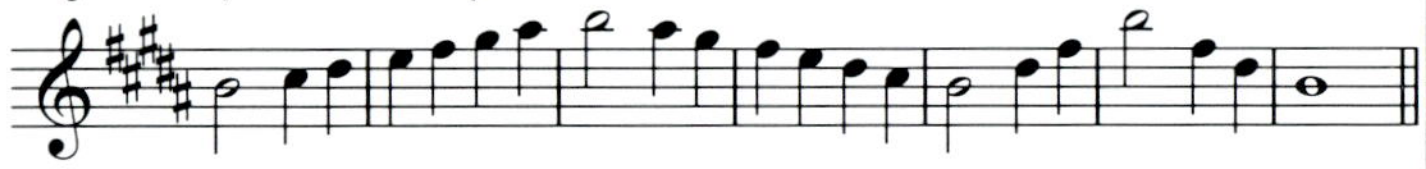

Key of F♯ (A Concert)

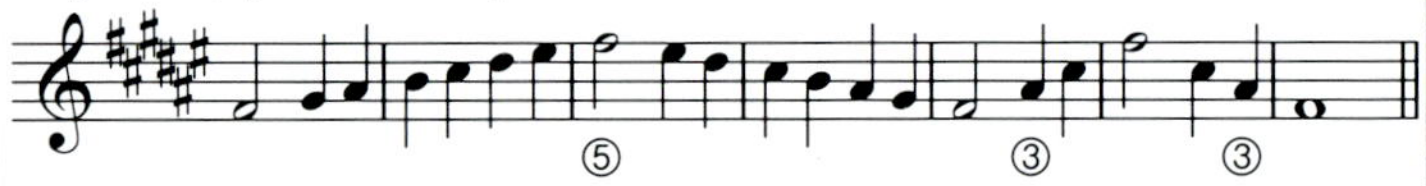

Key of D♭ (E Concert)

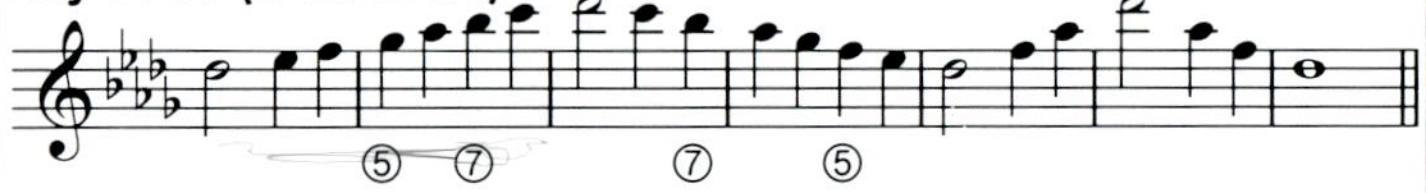

Minor Scales (Harmonic Mode) and Arpeggios

Key of E minor (G minor Concert)

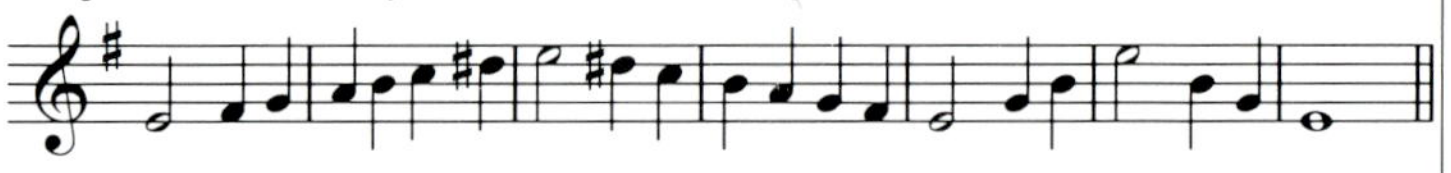

Key of A minor (C minor Concert)

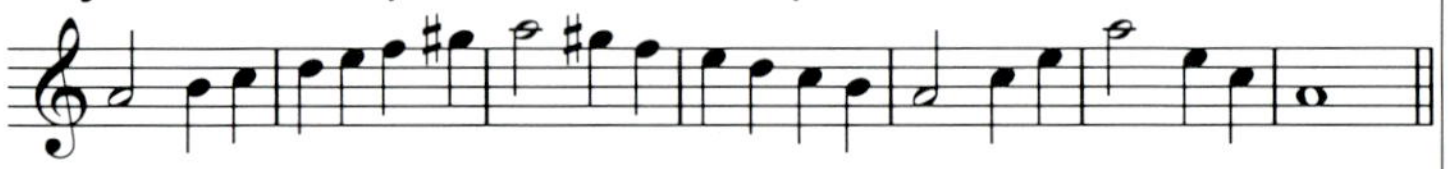

Key of D minor (F minor Concert)

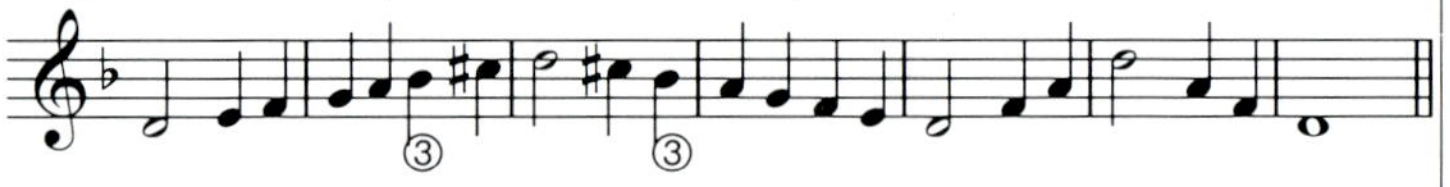

Key of G minor (B♭ minor Concert)

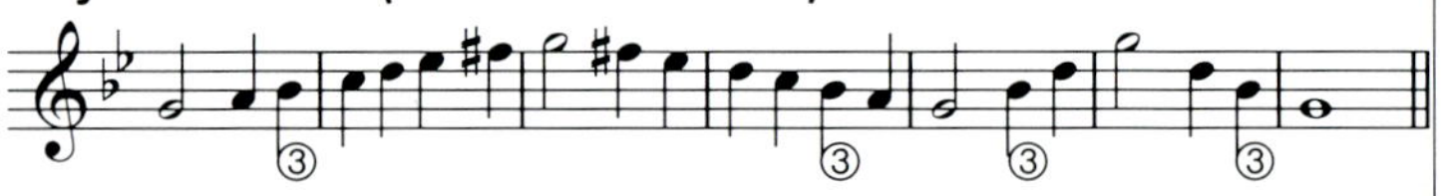

Key of C minor (E♭ minor Concert)

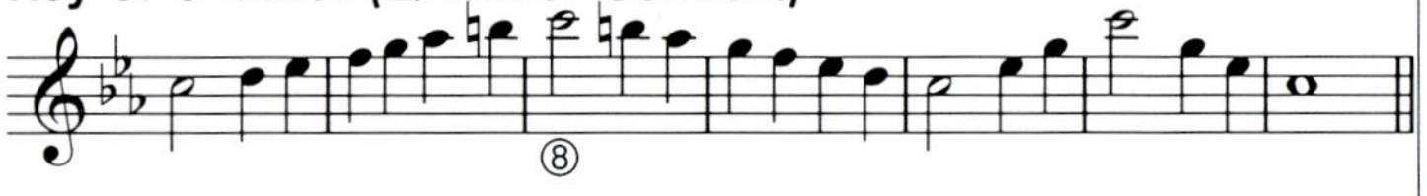

Key of F minor (A♭ minor Concert)

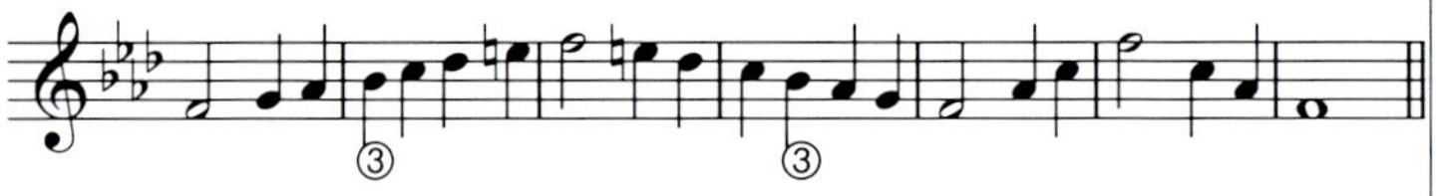

Key of B minor (D minor Concert)

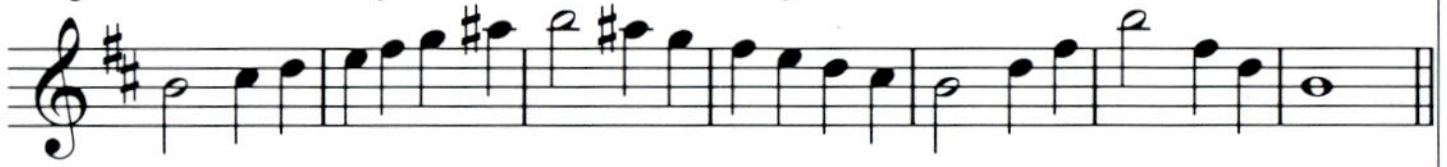

Key of F♯ minor (A minor Concert)

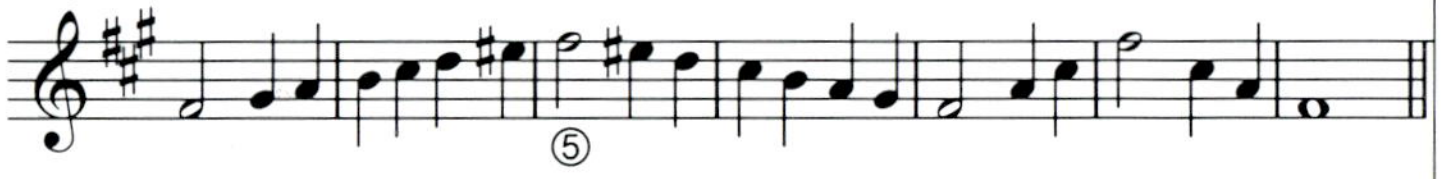

Key of C♯ minor (E minor Concert)

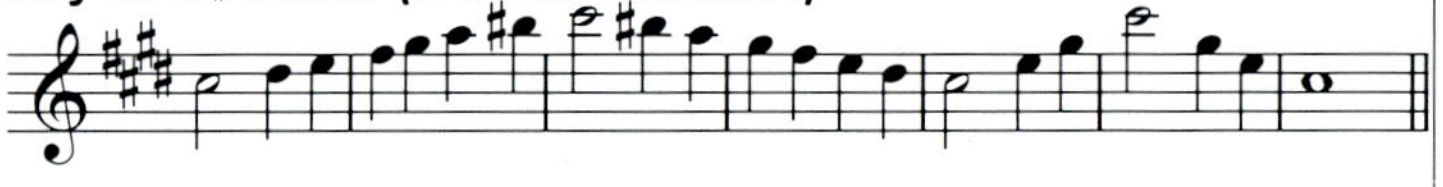

Key of A♭ minor (B minor Concert)

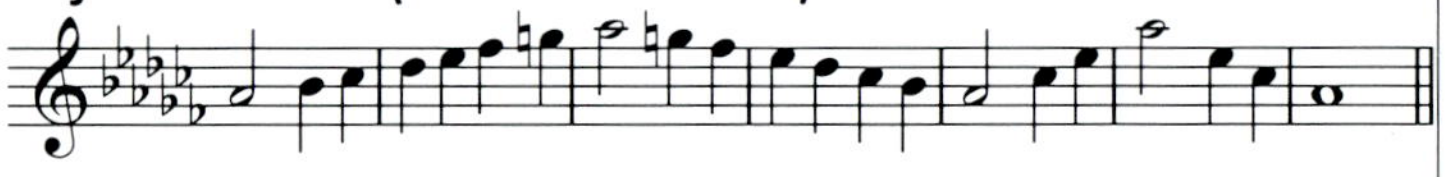

Key of E♭ minor (F♯ minor Concert)

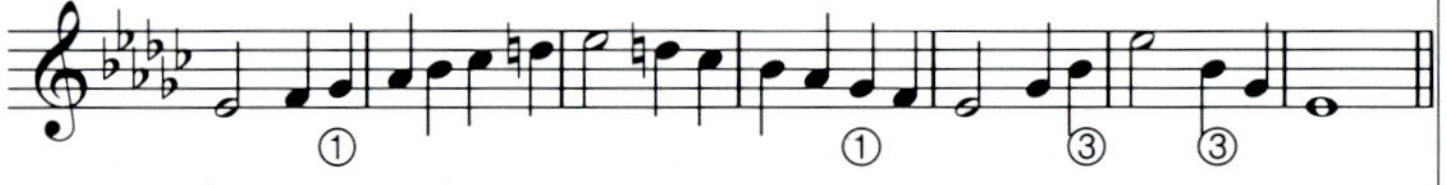

Key of B♭ minor (D♭ minor Concert)

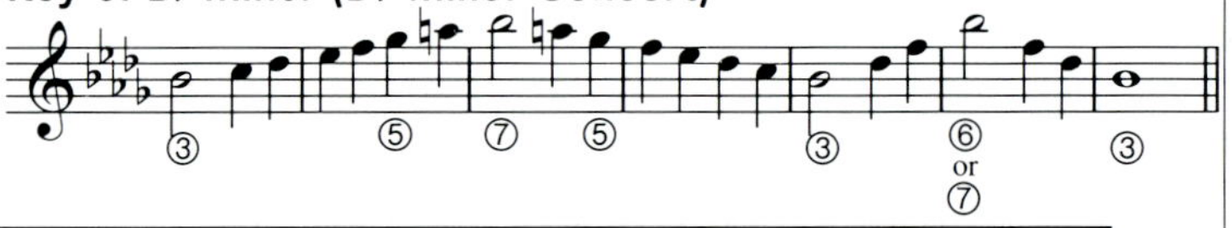

Chromatic Scale

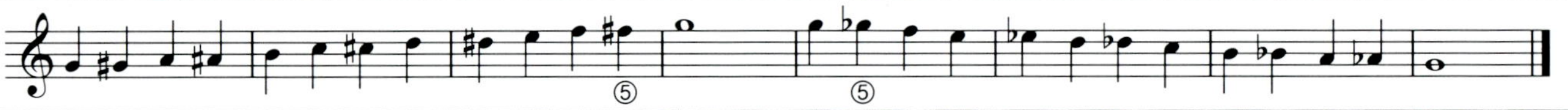

The circled number below a note refers to the recommended alternate fingering (see *Common Alternate Fingering chart*)

MB20396
$6.99 USD

ISBN 978-078-667-571-5